THE JUST STOP SERIES

The Simple & Quick Way to Get Rid of Any Bad Habit

**Ellie Izzo, PhD and
Vicki Carpol Miller, BSN, MS, LMFT**

Printed in the United States of America

 High Conflict Institute Press
High Conflict Institute, LLC
Scottsdale, Arizona

Book Design by www.KarrieRoss.com
Images from istockphoto.com

DEDICATED TO

Johnny and Skip who have lived with our
bad habits for years and still love us.

INTRODUCTION

Almost everyone, at one time or another in their lives, has had a bad habit. Some are easier than others to stop, but all of them have their roots in our deepest fears. Funny, but when we think about bad habits, fear is the last thing that comes to our minds because habits tend to bring us some false sense of comfort or relief. They make us feel better; but not really. They are all dangerous because they disconnect us from the power of our spirit—our true selves—and drain from us our real purpose for living.

The first six chapters of Just Stop Doing That will give you an understanding of what contributed to the development of your bad habits, and also will detail the five steps of the Rapid Advance Process.

This is a foundation necessary for you to complete Part Two, The Rapid Advance Workbook. By completing the workbook, we hope doors will open for you that empower you to rid yourself of these troublesome, annoying bad habits.

CONTENTS

Part One:

Part Two:

The Rapid Advance Workbook

PART ONE

CHAPTER ONE

Your Bad Habit Isn't Your Problem

It's Your Distraction

You have a higher mind. Everyone does. The ability to access your higher mind takes some energy on your part. When you are caught up in the vicious cycle of a bad habit, it is very challenging to think about the higher mind, much less connect to it. But we assure you there are states such as fulfillment and self control that are located in the upper part of your left brain which become easier to connect to with heightened awareness and a little bit of practice. When we refer to the spirit or higher mind, we mean that level of thinking ability that rises above stress and responds to scary situations with dynamics such as courage, faith, hope, trust and forgiveness. We want to be in our higher mind so we can use our rational thinking to deal with our negative emotional states. These negative emotional states are what drive our bad habits.

You are so invested in pouring time and energy into your bad habits, you forget about the option of creating better patterns through practicing higher thinking. Pity, because continuing in bad habits can only take you to very bad places. Uh oh! You better stop doing that!!

*Have you ever wondered what
you might be feeling if you stopped
your bad habit?*

Has anyone ever asked you about your bad habit? What excuses do you make? For example, why do you smoke? "Because it relaxes me and helps me to think." Why do you drink? "Because it takes the edge off a hard day." If your closet is full of new clothes and you're hiding new purchases under your bed, why do you continue to shop? "Because I love nice things." Why do you overeat? "Because I love good food." These are all denials, but excellent covers. These habits and many others are all distractions from what is truly ailing you. For example, if you are a smoker and you feel upset, your tendency is probably to "light up" rather than deal directly with your upset. Lighting up the cigarette distracts you from your upset, and in so doing, takes you away from your own internal power to face it and deal with it head on. If you are an overeater, you turn to food when you feel lonely. Food distracts you from your loneliness and separates you from your own inner ability to face your loneliness and move past it. This pattern holds true for any bad habit.

Have you ever wondered what you might be feeling if you stopped your bad habit? We believe that bad habits are formidable distractions from feeling afraid. After all, the world has become a scary place. War, economic crisis, terrorism, college shootings, crime, epidemics, biological warfare. We don't consciously ruminate about these things on a regular basis because our bad habits keep us at a distance from these sad realities. Television and other media bring us pictures and horrific stories within minutes of an event taking place. The Internet; YouTube; nothing is sacred. The scarier the better is how the world appears to be turning.

We don't want to get all scientific with you but some understanding of the human brain is very helpful when thinking about your bad habits. People who have incorporated bad habits into their lives operate in a fear-driven, mid-brain circuitry. The "bad habit" brain circuit burrows deeply and repetitively into the gray matter until it starts to resemble the configuration of a race track, deeply grooved and six lanes wide, and circular, with no exit. With each repetition of the bad habit, the grooves in the road get deeper and more entrenched and the possibilities of getting off the track are considerably less. "Bad habit neurons" race around the loop, making pit stops at the addiction receptors along the way, never getting off the track. The preferable way to get your brain to work is to build strong pathways to your spirit or higher mind where fear can be faced and overcome.

Not only will you have the opportunity to stop, but you will start receiving something far more satisfying instead.

It has become easy to give yourself over to the power of fear in a scary world by turning to a bad habit or two. We wonder if you can imagine yourself turning to courage, faith, and hope instead. We believe that connecting to your spirit or higher mind is a far more effective way to rise above your fears in life. Those of you stuck in bad habits need to consider how it is that you have forgotten about the power of your higher mind or have become disconnected from your spirit, because it is only by accessing the higher mind that you truly overcome your fears, stop your bad habits and experience satisfaction and peace in your daily life.

We don't want anything from you except your willing-ness to move through the five steps of the Rapid Advance Process, with the goal of stopping your bad habits. Not only will you have the opportunity to stop, but you will start receiving something far more satisfying instead.

We suspect that the thought of stopping your bad habit is scary in and of itself. After all, keeping that habit going has drained you of your energy, your time and your emotional well-being. So you may not think you have the strength to Just Stop Doing That! But, if you are tired of being a slave to your bad habit, we want to help you. If you have heard enough complaining from the people who care about you and who beg you to stop, we want to help you. We believe that this little book with our five simple steps has the ability to do so. Imagine yourself stopping your habit at the first thought you might engage in it. Picture yourself noticing your habit and moving away from it by taking it in a different direction. You would be in control of your habit—it would no longer be in control of you. Maybe you have tried therapy to help you with your bad habit, and it wasn't successful. Or, perhaps you couldn't afford to seek out a therapist. Maybe you have tried numerous recovery programs only to find yourself falling off the wagon within weeks or months. Just Stop Doing That! with the Rapid Advance Process provides five simple steps that you can do anywhere, anytime and on your own, using only your own mind.

How would you feel if you knew that your habit wasn't really your problem; that it was a distraction from something else far easier to overcome than the habit itself? Our goal is to help you discover your personal Impasse or that break from your essence or spirit. That point in your early experience where you began to feel afraid. Once you have recognized what you are afraid of, you can rid yourself of your bad habit and Stop Doing That. Now, let's get to work.

CHAPTER TWO

What in Heaven's Name Happened to You?

Revealing Your History

Your first response to the question, "What in heaven's name happened to you?" may be, "Nothing.", and we wouldn't be surprised if your answer was exactly that. That's why you have had habits. Our distractions or bad habits keep us separated (estranged) from our history.

We're not saying that your history is all bad, but the good stuff isn't of much interest at this point right now. We're only interested in identifying when you first started feeling afraid. Get a journal or pad of paper and start writing your autobiography. Start as early as you can remember and write about your childhood, your family, your school, your friends and anything significant that happened to you. Write your history as if it were a narrative or story. Take your time. Pay attention and don't leave stuff out. You will orchestrate your own story, making it as detailed or as long as you would like.

When the pathway to your spirit is blocked,
or develops an Impasse, you "hit the wall"
and have no choice other than to retreat
back to the race track of fear—you know,
the one we spoke of earlier.

You didn't come into this world feeling afraid. You were born a little ball of love, precious and innocent until life started happening to you. Your Ego (the part of you that you show the world, and that which is separated from your spiritual self) began developing as a defense against feeling afraid. You may think that your personal childhood history holds no triggers or truly upsetting events, but in reality, your childhood holds the key to the development of your bad habits. Many of us have forgotten much of the past or perhaps have developed a selective recall about it. We are not suggesting that you get bogged down in your past, but reviewing it has merit. This review provides an opportunity to use your history as a catalyst to make positive changes in the here and now.

We are interested in how your judgment or perception of some of your historical events may have caused this break, or as we call it, an Impasse, to your spirit. This Impasse doesn't allow you to access the part of your brain that houses the qualities of courage, strength, forgiveness, faith and hope. When the pathway to your spirit is blocked, or develops an Impasse, you "hit the wall" and have no choice other than to retreat back to the race track of fear—you know, the one we spoke of earlier. This negatively affects your belief system and causes you to feel afraid. You then turn to your bad habit to distract and falsely soothe yourself.

Samantha the Smoker

Samantha, a 40-year-old woman, shared the following experience when revealing her history. As a young child of 4, Samantha and her mother went on an excursion to New York City. They took the train and spent the day wandering the streets and window shopping.

Samantha's Mom took her to a cafeteria for lunch. Samantha was fascinated by the walls full of little windows behind which stood an array of beautiful desserts like lemon meringue pie and delicious entrees like spaghetti and meatballs. Her mother gave her a handful of quarters, allowing her to choose on her own, any and all of her lunch selections.

Samantha had a blast putting in the quarters, opening the little glass doors to retrieve her goodies. The day ended on a pleasant note and she slept soundly when she got into her little bed. The next morning, when Samantha and her mother were in the front yard, a neighbor came by to chat. Samantha's mother began to recount the big trip into the city of New York, and Samantha chimed in with, "…and we had so much fun at the cafeteria!"

Samantha's mother motioned for her to go back into the house, which she did gladly. She was watching television when her mother stormed in and approached her, pulling her hand back and slapping her across the face while she seethed, "Don't you ever embarrass me in front of the neighbors ever again."

Samantha had no idea what she had said wrong. Samantha had no idea that lunch at the cafeteria was considered by her mother to be a place to eat that was "beneath her." Her little spirit was broken, and at the time, she didn't know why. She didn't realize that her precious innocence was demoralized and not until she was an adult did she understand or even remember the incident. She recalls that in order to sooth her broken spirit, she would suck her thumb whenever she felt afraid or sad. She remembers her mother saying, "Stop sucking your thumb. You'll get buck teeth." Samantha's bad habit of thumb-sucking transitioned into smoking as an adult.

You decided and judged early on that certain people, places and things were big and scary. You didn't like that feeling of fear so you buried it, or did something else to cope with it. Those coping mechanisms or distractions, helped soothe your fears while you navigated through your childhood. You might have sucked your thumb, had nightmares, or wet your bed. Perhaps you had temper tantrums, were painfully shy, or aggressive with other children. Maybe you did poorly in school, daydreamed or stared out the window. Maybe you got sick a lot. Perhaps you were too competitive or not competitive enough. Take a minute and remember some of your childhood behaviors. They were the seedlings of behaviors you possess today. Some of them are helpful to you; some of them are bad habits that keep you from connecting to your spirit or higher mind.

What is important to understand is that no matter how large or small the habit, overcoming it is equally straightforward for everyone.

As a child, when you started to feel fear, you developed what we refer to as Impasses; roadblocks to the pathways that take you to your spirit or higher mind. Fear creates an Impasse for a child and stops the child's ability to connect to the precious higher state of their innocence. Think back to a time when you were young and you felt anxious, afraid or sad. How did you comfort yourself? Soothing or distracting behaviors, which can become habits, help the child survive and relieve the feelings of fear. A child typically looks to a parent to help with their fear, but sometimes, the parent is the one who is causing the fear. Maybe your parents didn't realize that you were scared. They may have reacted to your distracting behaviors with criticism or neglect. It wasn't their fault. Don't forget, just like everyone else, they were operating with their own distractions to remain unconscious of their own childhood fears.

Many parents become focused on their child's distracting behavior, thinking it is the problem when in reality it is the child's solution to feeling afraid—the only way the child knows how to deal with the fear or the Impasse.

As a child, when you started to feel fear, you developed what we refer to as Impasses; roadblocks to the pathways that take you to your spirit or higher mind.

The emotional blueprint from your childhood Impasses can set the stage for the development of bad habits in your adulthood. As you start to grow you begin to experience fear. The way a child copes with fear is by distracting him or herself from it. These distractions root themselves into your behavior patterns and set the stage for bad habits that are difficult to stop as you become an adult. What is important to understand is that no matter how large or small the habit, overcoming it is equally straightforward for everyone. You simply need to acknowledge that the Impasse occurred and then, make the personal commitment to face it, allowing you to reconnect to the power of your spirit or higher mind.

Hungry Harrison

Harrison was a binge eater. He was hungry all the time. He tried to curb his appetite, but when he started to eat, he simply could not stop. He boasted that he "never met a meal he didn't like." He also boasted that he had lost thousands of pounds over the course of his adult life by going on trendy diets, but always managed to gain the weight back and then some.

When Harrison was young, he witnessed a lot of fighting between his parents. His father would end up storming out of the house and be gone for many hours and sometimes for days. His mother would retreat into her bedroom and close the door. After what seemed to Harrison to be hours of sobbing, all would go quiet and she remained sequestered for many hours.

Needless to say, Harrison spent a lot of time by himself. He remembers knocking on his mother's bedroom door very quietly and receiving no response. This would frighten him, but he was even more afraid of knocking harder and upsetting his mother even more. So he would go into the kitchen and eat everything in sight between his periods of quiet knocking on her door. By the time Harrison entered into first grade he was thirty pounds overweight. His parents told him,

"Stop eating all that junk food, Harrison. You're really getting chubby." But comforting himself during their conflicts through overeating was Harrison's self-soothing behavior or distraction. As an adult, Harrison found it hard to ever be alone, and continued to swallow his fear in food.

Whether your fears from childhood are a dark closet, being bullied by a scary kid, being caught in the rain, coming home from school and having no one in the house, being disciplined, hearing strange noises, having nightmares, losing a friend, losing a love, going through a divorce, having an accident, feeling publicly embarrassed in school or in front of the family, becoming ill and missing out on important activities, shyness in school, moving a lot, just to name a few. They are stored. When these historical feelings are triggered by something in the present, you are at risk to turn to your bad habit as a way to cope.

We suggest that there is an alternative.

CHAPTER THREE

Hitting the Wall!

Recognizing Your Impasse

Now that you have revealed your history, you are ready to recognize your Impasse or that place in your experience where an early fear becomes triggered in the here and now. When you are triggered, you "hit the wall", similar to what happens to an athlete when they are performing at their absolute best and then experience a complete stop due to exhaustion of his or her internal resources. When you are triggered in the present, you emotionally hit the wall, because the current trigger is related in some way to the past event that caused you to feel fearful. Just like a small child, you perceive that you have no internal resources to overcome the fear and so you shut down and retreat into your bad habit.

Some common Impasses that make you feel afraid are:

- abandonment
- being hurt
- inferiority or not being good enough
- commitment
- not being lovable
- loss of competence
- failure
- success
- the unknown
- losing control
- death
- divorce
- and numerous others

Hungry Harrison, perceiving himself as left alone by his parents, developed a fear of abandonment. He swallowed this fear through overeating. Samantha the Smoker developed a fear of being hurt with no forewarning, as a result of witnessing her mother's unpredictable reactions. She sucked her thumb to relax her mind. When you look closely at your personal situation, you can identify your own personal fears. You will write them down later in the Workbook section following your personal history.

Peggy The Procrastinator

Peggy was the head of the language department at a local community college. She had worked at this job for over 20 years, even though she complained about it and always spoke of looking for better positions which she never got around to doing.

She rarely graded her papers on time and found herself staying up until 2 or 3 a.m. the night before an exam day, preparing last minute exam questions for her students. She had a storage unit parked outside in her back yard filled with stacks of papers accumulated over years of teaching, just waiting for Peggy to have the time to sort them—a time which never came.

Peggy was the last born and only daughter in a family with two older brothers. Her father was a civil engineer and demanded perfection from his children while he gave special praise to his sons. Peggy was left to the care of a loving but very quiet, fade into the background kind of mother. Even though she graduated at the top of her class with special honors in foreign language, she never felt she made the grade in the eyes of her father.

Her Impasse, fear of inferiority, was brought on by an incident she recalled that took place at age 16. Her father told her that after she was late in repaying a debt to him, she was incompetent at prioritizing what was important in life. He told her, "Stop putting things off, Peggy. Other people would think that you're lazy and irresponsible." She internalized this critical

*comment and continued her procrastination regarding
all aspects of her life, fearing she could never live up to
what others needed from her.*

Your Impasse is the key to understanding and stopping your bad habit. Remember, history repeats itself.
Those of us who have unresolved fears from the past are
at risk to have these fears come up again and again.
We see them rear their ugly heads in our primary
relationships, our parenting, in our workplace and friendships. This happens outside of our awareness and we end
up innocently projecting our childhood fears onto other
important people in our lives.

*Those of us who have unresolved
fears from the past are at risk to have
these fears come up again and again.*

The distractions of our childhood "have matured".
A thumb sucker may have developed into a drug abuser;
a painfully shy child may develop into a workaholic to
avoid involvement in meaningful relationships. A little
more sophisticated, but distractions all the same. We stay
stuck in the past with the help of our adult habits because
we are unconsciously pre-wired to do so. Once our history has been revealed, we are able to recognize how we set
up the Impasse again and again in adulthood. We've been
doing it for so long, we don't even notice it.

Susie the Shopper

When Susie was a young girl, she lived in what was considered in her community to be a successful and prosperous family. When she was in her early teens, her Dad lost his job and this wealthy family then went through some very hard times. She heard many arguments between her parents leading up to and resulting in a difficult divorce where they fought over every remaining penny.

One day Susie went to the mall with her girlfriends. As she went to buy some clothes from her favorite store, and handed the cashier her credit-card, she was horrified when the charges were declined. The humiliation she felt in front of her teenage friends was received by Susie as a break to her spiritual connection. She saw herself as "less than" because the family was in financial trouble and now, everyone knew!

She moved on from that situation with a silent fear of scarcity and poverty. As an adult, she developed the bad habit of compulsive shopping when this scarcity fear became triggered. This bad habit became so intrusive into her life, she secretly purchased another home into which she crowded all the thousands of items she had purchased over time. Susie was a stay at home Mom and a very loving force in her family yet no one knew about this secret part of her life. She was lonely and felt afraid that if her husband found out, he would certainly leave her.

When you are operating from an internal place of fear, your relationships with others become tainted and you establish fear-based connections rather than love-based connections. Pretty soon, you and the other are both collaborating in fear and the only way to go is downhill. Getting a handle on your fears and recognizing the Impasse your fear has caused will allow you to better relate to those important people in your lives.

Many of you were raised in codependent families where you watched one parent caretaking or managing the other. The message that gets hardwired into the developing brain of a child who sees this is that managing or controlling the other is more important than staying clear and centered with oneself. The sad reality is that every time a person manages or controls the other, they have accidentally denied the other an important opportunity to manage him or herself. We see this, commonly, in addictive families where the spouse of the addicted person manages the addict. We also see it in domestic abuse where the spouse of a habitual rager manages the mood of the rager rather than support him or her in controlling his or her own temper.

Furthermore, if you were raised in these fear-based styles, they become your Impasse and you unintentionally repeat these patterns in your adult relationships. This can create the dreaded "woe- is- me" bad habit, a victim position that is very tempting and extremely difficult to break free from simply because victims are rarely expected to be accountable or responsible. The "woe-is-me" bad habit may seem like an easy way out of a scary situation.

But this so-called easy way becomes the hard way when you realize that victims are also perceived as helpless and powerless to take any control over the quality of their lives. This habit of helplessness attracts to the victim exactly what he/she does not need—either an attacker or a rescuer.

When you are operating from an internal place of fear, your relationships with others become tainted and you establish fear-based connections rather than love-based connections.

It is essential for you to identify the earlier feeling of helplessness from your original break to the spirit. Then, and only then, can you choose to mend this break.

William the Woeful One

William, a medical doctor, worked all the time. He always chose to be on call even though his partners offered to share this responsibility with him. He would start his rounds at 6 o'clock every morning. He would see patients at his office from 9 in the morning to 7 at night and then he would teach at the local medical school several evenings per week. William was wonderful in his work but his mood changed dramatically when he walked through his front door. William would work himself into total exhaustion and then take his anger at himself out on his wife when he returned home after a long day. His wife said, "Of course you're tired. Stop working so hard." But William always had an excuse about why that wasn't possible.

Revealing William's history helped him to get a handle on this situation. He was the firstborn in a family of 4 children. His mother was an invalid who was chronically sick, in bed all the time, barking orders from her sickbed. To this day, no one is certain about exactly what, if anything was wrong with her.

William's father dedicated his entire life to nursing his wife and her chronically poor health set the tone as to how William's family life would play out. The children were expected to keep quiet and take care of themselves, lest their mother have a setback. His father had no needs in the marriage because it would be absurd to expect anything from a partner who was unable to function.

William remembered feeling cheated and ignored as a child. He had no relationship with his mother, and felt trapped in being cooperative with his father's need to play nurse. William had recreated the Impasse on several levels—choosing a career as a doctor seemed logical after revealing his history. The choice to work ridiculously long hours and to ask for nothing within his marriage also fits. His bad habit of over-working helped keep William distracted from the painful Impasse: he must suffer in silence in order to feel worthy.

Once you recognize the Impasse as you set it up in the present, you might notice that you move around in a chronic state of separation anxiety. Separation Anxiety refers to the upset a child feels when he or she must detach from a parent. Consider this thought; what if separation anxiety is actually the chronic underlying distress you feel as a result of being separated from the most loving and nurturing spiritual part of YOURSELF? If this is true, we remain separated by fear in adulthood and stick to certain bad habits as a way to avoid feeling this unpleasant anxiety. Imagine what might happen if you were to recognize and then meet this anxiety head on. Then, maybe your bad habit would no longer serve a purpose.

Look at the underlying and silent themes from your family in order to recognize your Impasse. Many times these themes appear subtle and unimportant in your grown up point of view. For example, in some families boys are treated differently than girls. In other families, some religious practices crowd out healthy and direct communication. Money issues, changing values, and family secrets can all contribute to creating Impasses.

In other situations, how others saw the family might have been more important than what was truly happening within it. In recognizing your Impasse, don't always look for the obvious. Many times it is the unspoken theme or code of silence that can drive the Impasse forward, sometimes for generations.

If you remain attached to the past by fear, you are destined to continue in your bad habits. Attachment to the past through fear has an addictive quality to it; the familiarity of being stuck at the Impasse has a perverse sense of comfort simply because you are so used to being fearful and anxious and you remain attached to the associated separation anxiety we spoke of earlier. Comfortably uncomfortable is one way to think of this.

By recognizing when you are replaying an updated version in the present of a scary historical scene from the past, you can then experience rather than avoid the separation anxiety that gets triggered in the replay. If you can do this, you are at the gateway of stopping your bad habits. Recognizing your Impasse is your wake-up call to experience your separation from your loving self or spirit. When you begin the journey of reconnecting to your spirit, you will know that you are not abandoned and therefore never really alone.

CHAPTER FOUR

Cutting Loose the Ball and Chain!

Releasing the Past

We now understand that when we remain attached to the past, we cannot connect to our innocent spiritual self or higher mind. As long as we are in disconnect, we are operating from an underlying sense of fear. We then revert back to the coping skills of our childhood by distracting ourselves from feeling afraid. Being connected to our spiritual self-empowers us to stay peacefully centered in the here and now.

Once you have revealed your history, recognized your personal Impasse, and made the decision to no longer retreat from fear through your bad habit, you can now begin to access your higher mind or spiritual self. To do this, you must release the past by learning how to forgive.

Memories are not really the past;
they are only perceptions of it.

In the beginning this might be experienced as a challenge because you are in the midst of separation anxiety at the time you call upon yourself to *Just Stop Doing That!* However, what is different now is that you can take a leap of faith that in stopping your habit, you can find your way back to your spirit, that part of you that was broken at an earlier point in your life. As we give fear over to our spiritual mind, we receive spiritual traits in ourselves like courage, patience and peacefulness.

Take a moment to define the past. Some define it as *the time before or time gone by*. What does that mean? The past is a span of time. Is it real? Is it something you can hold on to? We don't think so. Your memories of time gone by are all that really exist now and they exist only in your mind. Memories are not really the past; they are only perceptions of it. Have you ever experienced an event with another person where you were present for the same period of time in that shared situation, and later, you both recalled the incident differently? It is important to realize that *what* you remember is far less impacting that *how* you remember. The historical action is over. It is only your judgment of it that actually remains.

A father's memory of his family may be very different from his child's. The father may remember the family situation to have been wonderful with his role as very positive and helpful. His child's perception may be infinitely different. The child may remember the relationship with the father to have been, at times, unsafe. Perhaps when the father was angry, he was perceived by his child as a scary guy.

Now we ask you, who was right and who was wrong? Neither? Both? When this child decides to release the past, he or she understands that the existing memory of the father's behavior was simply one point of view. When this same child overcomes or rises above his fear of that upsetting or scary situation, he also relinquishes *his personal judgment* about his lovability in the eyes of that scary parent.

When you release judgment of the past,
you have released the past itself.

The point is that a perception of your past exists in your mind and that is all there is left of it. The events themselves are much less meaningful than how you took in the events as they occurred. How you took them in, experienced them, processed them, and judged yourself in the context of them is what makes up your perception of them.

You can change your perception any time you choose to let go of or release your judgment of the past. When you release judgment of the past, you have released the past itself.

Homophobic Henry

Henry finally decided he was in a bad habit of gay bashing when his continued derogatory remarks about gay people cost him an important loving 5-year relationship with his girlfriend. She had asked him repeatedly to "Just Stop Doing That!" and when she realized he couldn't stop, she broke off the relationship. Henry was devastated and decided that if he didn't stop this habit, he may never find a love.

Henry revealed his history. Once, when he was about 6 years old, he went crying to his stepfather because his younger sister had grabbed a doll he was playing with and took it away from him. His stepfather became enraged and yelled at Henry, "You're nothing but a sissy!" Adding insult to injury, he forced Henry to wear a dress to school every day for a week. He was teased. He was tormented. People called him derogatory names. Henry felt frightened and ashamed. He grew up feeling fearful about any healthy feminine traits he possessed. He distracted himself from this fear through the bad habit of gay bashing.

To release the past, Henry had to let go of his judgment of this memory and of his stepfather. While the stepfather had no doubt believed he was teaching

Henry a valuable social lesson, Henry took in the experience quite differently. In releasing the past, Henry had to understand that his lingering painful memory is no longer about his stepfather. It is really about the judgment Henry carried about himself in this situation and his perception of his stepfather's behavior. His stepfather might have been homophobic or worried about how others would perceive of him having a son who played with dolls.

Every time Henry engaged in his habit of attacking gay people, he was ultimately attacking himself for his own healthy feminine side, thereby digging himself deeper and deeper into his Impasse; an Impasse which actually cost him a loving heterosexual relationship.

Some of you have a self-definition that is based on what those who cared for you told you about yourself. If you were told over and over that you were cute, ugly, smart, stupid, clumsy, graceful, fat, skinny, a sissy, a jock, etc., these remarks could have become a foundation for your identity. They may have gotten in the way of your fulfillment in exploring and discovering *on your own* who you wanted to be and what was important to you. Imagine if you were free of those judgments and intrusions into your development, who might you choose to be? Write it down in your workbook.

Now we realize that there are those of you who are stuck at the Impasse and we hear the balking. "Right, ladies, my father beat me to a pulp with his belt and

I have a faulty perception of it." Yes, your father did beat you with a belt and it appears he is still doing it, only now, he has your permission to do so. You see, the beating itself no longer exists. The beating hurt you physically at the time it happened. It was very painful. Today, only your perception of it remains.

Once again we repeat: release your judgment of a scary memory and the memory no longer carries the emotional weight it once did.

Try to grasp this concept. The beating itself never had any meaning. (We know this is difficult to grasp/understand, but hang on, we will explain.) The way you felt about yourself at the time it happened is now the only remaining meaning the beating has. How did you feel when you were being beaten? Afraid? Sad? Shameful? Angry? These are words that may describe your feelings. What have you done about these feelings? One thing you've done is distract yourself through a bad habit. Another is that you haven't been able to release this particular aspect of your past and move forward. You may have projected these feelings onto other important people or relationships in your life. These distracting behaviors or bad habits detract from the loving quality of your significant relationships and don't solve the problem of the underlying pain you hold on to. Once again we repeat: release your judgment of a scary memory and the memory no longer carries the emotional weight it once did. Being beaten by your father was bad when he did it, but it isn't bad now, because it isn't happening now. It just was.

Allen The Assaulted One

Allen had developed a terrible habit of drinking too much. It was a blissful escape from facing the responsibilities of work and family. His wife complained bitterly and he drank more in response. When she finally moved out and yelled, "Just Stop Doing That!" he decided to do some self-reflection.

Allen grew up in the Midwest and was the older of two children. Both parents were active alcoholics as far back as he could remember. His father did most of his drinking away from home and when he did drink at home, it was when the family socialized and it was all in good fun. His mother, on the other hand, was a mean and nasty drunk. She would really tie one on when the father was away at one of his frequent business trips. She would take Allen and his sister, leave them sitting in the car in town while she drank for hours at the local bar.

Allen excelled at anything he attempted whether it was friendships, academics, sports or jobs. He was well known in the town as the local golden boy in the area of sports and was written up in the paper on a weekly basis for his accomplishments in the high school sports program.

Allen revealed one terrifying incident when a friend stopped by at the family dinner hour and was invited by

Allen's mother to stay and eat. His mother had been drinking since early afternoon and when Allen made a defensive remark about his father's absence, his mother became violent and full of rage. She grabbed her fork, stabbing Allen in his forearm, leaving it standing up while his friend looked on in horror. He also recalled having to sleep with one eye open and a kitchen knife under his pillow, as his mother would come in during the night and threaten to kill him if he went to sleep.

Allen's Impasse was a fear of death that when triggered, causing him to "hit the wall" emotionally. He began drinking heavily as a way to escape that overwhelming fear. He was able to release his past by working on forgiveness of his parents, particularly his mother.

You may often tend to blame your parents for the misery you continue to experience as an adult. You are at risk to see yourself as a victim. You might even start to believe that unless your parents fix it or apologize, you will remain forever at the mercy of their crimes. That is when you turn to your habit to distract yourself feelings of fear and powerlessness. But are you powerless now?

Consider this. It's not about your parents anymore. Now it is all about you and your perceptions of them, and yourself in relation to them. Continuing to blame or judge parents, or anyone else for that matter, is just another distraction from your chronic fear. Allen could spend a lifetime blaming his mother and father for abandoning him and causing him great fear and anxiety. He could blame them for his drinking habit and for taking away his innocence and giftedness. Or, he could choose to forgive them, releasing himself from the stronghold these memories have on his life.

Forgiveness, the relinquishment of judgment followed by a thought of peace, is the path to recovery from bad habits and lifelong pain.

How do you change your fearful perceptions of past events so that you can release them and reconnect to the power of your spirit? Through forgiveness, that's how.

Forgiveness, the relinquishment of judgment followed by a thought of peace, is the path to recovery from bad habits and lifelong pain. Without forgiveness, you will always be stopped at your Impasse, finding it impossible to connect to your spirit and your higher mind. For Allen, it was realizing that he was always deserving of a loving mother, even though he lived with a sick and tortured woman. He recognized that as long as he carried his childhood fear of her in the here and now, he could never move forward to realize his gifts and talents. He was not being threatened in the present. His mother's violent acts and threats happened in the past. As long as he kept inspiring the memory, she continued to stab him with fear.

Allen worked on forgiving his mother by relinquishing his judgment of her violent behavior and thinking about her with peace. He also forgave himself for mistakenly believing he was an unlovable child because of the parents he was born to.

How do you relinquish judgment of someone else or yourself for a painful mistake? Ask yourself this question, "How would I experience this differently if I considered it from a position of love rather than fear?" In other words, "How would my spirit have me know this?" The pain of a scary childhood event can be overwhelming from a position of fear. It can also disappear when you release it with forgiveness.

Forgiveness is for people, not for actions. When you are faced with an awful mistake, be it your own or someone else's, it would be far more effective to forgive yourself and/or the other person and give the mistake over to your higher mind. This relinquishment invites wisdom in to handle the problem. When forgiveness is practiced this way, watch the course of events that follow work in a way to rectify the mistake. The same holds true for a bad habit. Holding on to judgment about a scary event keeps breathing life into the event so that in our perception it is happening over and over again. This then drives the repetitive nature of distracting yourself through your bad habit. Please *Just Stop Doing That!*

Take some time now and reflect upon some memory that has resulted in a negative self judgment. It does not necessarily need to be as dramatic as some of the examples used in this book in order to illustrate a particular point. Maybe someone in your past contributed to the story of your identity by helping you to believe you are something that you would prefer not to be. You can shift your perception of that memory right now by stating, "That memory is not bad. It just is. Now, what do I want to create for myself around it?" Releasing the past through the relinquishment of judgment begins breaking down your Impasse and opening the pathways to your spirit or your higher mind. Now, you are ready to use thoughts of peace to stop your bad habits when you are being challenged by fear.

CHAPTER FIVE

You Don't Scare Me!

Responding To Fear

There is a big difference between responding and reacting. Reacting involves little or no spiritual connection.
It is automatic and falls into the race track circuitry of
your lower brain functioning. Reactions are defensive in
nature and based on your primitive instincts of fight or
flight. You react when you have a need to protect yourself.
Sometimes this is desirable. If a car is coming right at
you, hopefully you will react by swerving your own
vehicle out of the way. In a situation where you are immediately threatened, the fight or flight instinct kicks in
automatically. Reaction skills are very useful should you
find yourself in physically dangerous circumstances.

Responding to fear rather than reacting to it supports your release of the past.

Responding, on the other hand, involves the thoughtful preparation of a reply. How do you respond in emotionally fearful conditions? Do you light a cigarette or have a drink to ready yourself? Do you avoid attending to those emotionally charged situations by putting off what is inevitable? If you learn to respond, rather than react in emotionally scary circumstances, you will not need to fight or flee. You will be able to remain present and accountable.

Responding to fear rather than reacting to it supports your release of the past. Once you have relinquished the judgment around an earlier event, you need to stay peaceful when you meet up with a scary present day situation that triggers your fear. You have already committed to let go of the past. You have committed to no longer perceive yourself as a victim of it. When fear is triggered you can now recognize that you are at your Impasse. You can now consider healthier options rather than turn back to your bad habit in order to cope. You can choose to rise above your separation anxiety and remember that you are not abandoned and that you are not alone.

There is nothing missing in you; nothing you need to get; nothing you need to buy. You have everything you need; all the precious parts of yourself are already there. You have simply been detached from it until now. Your spiritual self is showing up; not your fear-driven, scared little child. Your spiritual self is showing up with thoughtfulness, courage, peace and faith in your ability to move forward.

Belligerent Betty

*Betty had a terrible habit of being rude to people, short-tempered and impatient. She was belligerent and came on strong to just about anyone who crossed her path. She reacted defensively in the most benign interactions. This habit had already cost her two good jobs and several relationships. In her last job, her co-workers were setting all kinds of boundaries with her and complaining repeatedly to her supervisor. She realized she would have to **Just Stop Doing That** if she wanted to have any meaningful dimension to her life.*

Betty revealed her history. In her early adolescence, her father announced that he was leaving her mother for another woman. He moved out. Two weeks later, Betty came home from middle school to find that her mother had sold their home that very morning and was leaving immediately for an extended worldwide trip. Betty was spontaneously emancipated from her family. Her life and her living arrangements instantly became her responsibility, ready or not.

Obviously, Betty wasn't ready. She looked up a distant cousin who lived on the other side of town and moved in to her home so she could finish school. In order to get by, she had to take a part time job. This was the beginning of Betty's fear of abandonment and her perception of herself as a "have-not". If anyone ever knew that she was such a "loser" they would never want to associate with her.

Betty was so afraid of rejection, she was purposely combative or nasty to keep people away. Betty recognized this break to her spirit which occurred at the time of her parents' divorce. As she utilized forgiveness to release her past, she noticed herself becoming more capable of responding rather than reacting to her historical fear when it was triggered. She then built a close relationship with her cousin and other nice people in the neighborhood. She was able to forgive her parents for their erratic and irresponsible behavior toward her and realized that they were so afraid of their own marital abandonment; they forgot to consider the losses of their young daughter.

As she utilized the dynamic of forgiveness by relinquishing judgment around how her parents handled their divorce, and wishing them peace, she noticed herself more energized to respond rather than react to her historical fear when it was triggered in her life. She also realized that she was worthy of love and of good parenting, even though her parents made extremely poor choices during a traumatic time in their lives.

Have you ever felt afraid or insecure in a relationship? What is that fear about? Why are you afraid? Take some time right now and think about the answers to these questions and write them down.

When these fears are triggered, how do you react so you don't have to feel the fear? Emotional reacting occurs as a result of poor impulse control. Your immediate impulse is to get away from the scary feeling because it is unpleasant. You impulsively turn to your bad habits which gives fear power over your life. You also abandon yourself when you turn to your bad habits by dishonoring what you are really feeling. Instead, you distract yourself from the feeling with a bad habit that gets out of control and helps you to believe that you are not very competent at functioning in the world. Acknowledging your fear is required in order to respond to it.

Acknowledging your fear is required in order to respond to it.

Responding is a discipline that requires a lot of practice to become good at it. Responding to fear is best developed by following three behavioral steps: **Stop, Look and Listen**. Do you remember this phrase being taught to you as a child when learning to cross the street? Some streets may be easier to cross than others. How many streets have you crossed where you never bothered to stop, look and listen? At some of the scary intersections, you could be easily mowed down if you didn't follow the rules. When you find yourself at a frightening emotional intersection, the rule of responding is to Stop! Look! And Listen! Let's start with Stop!

Identify what will become your personal red light. When you're struggling with a bad habit, it is easy to identify your personal red light. For a smoker, it would be the thought of lighting up. For a drinker, it would be the thought of pouring a drink. For a procrastinator, it would be the thought of doing something else rather than what needs to be done. Ironically, you will find yourself at a place where your biggest problem, your bad habit, becomes your greatest reminder to respond rather than react to what is going on.

Just keep this advice in mind when you are identifying your personal red light: never tell yourself statements like, "I don't know" or "I'm trying" as you begin to develop this skill. The statements "I don't know" and "I'm trying" are very popular distractions to avoid dealing with fear. They are actually a serious form of self-abandonment that will keep you stuck in the victim position, will strengthen your Impasse, and leave you feeling powerless and hopeless.

It is okay and makes perfect sense that you would experience fear in letting go.

There is really no such thing as "trying" when you are making choices for positive change. You are either doing it or not doing it. You don't have to be hard on yourself when you are not doing it, but at least be honest about it.

When you ask yourself the hard questions about your bad habit, the answer, "I don't know" is only reinforcing your underlying struggle of unworthiness and undermines your ability to respond to fear. Of course you know why, but if you admitted to it, you'd then take on the responsibility of making a healthy change. If you're afraid to look at why, simply say so as the first step in stopping your bad habit. Stop and honor your feeling of fear. It is okay and makes perfect sense that you would experience fear in letting go.

You always know in your heart of hearts what is going on with you. Stuck at the Impasse, you might be afraid to look at it. Once you have stopped the bad habit, you free yourself to look inward and reveal your truth in what is happening. Again, we ask you the question, "Why are you afraid to let go of your bad habit?" Now listen to your truth. Please don't answer with "I don't know." You do know. Just take some time and sit with that feeling long enough to really feel it. If you would dare to stay with that scary feeling for as long as it takes, you will soon discover what it means to you. One thing we have experienced in our years of work is that legitimate feelings such as fear or sadness are self-limiting and do not spin out of control when they are faced. However, the distractions we use to ovoid these legitimate feelings can and do often spin out of control. Listen to your answer. It deserves to be heard.

For Samantha, looking into her fear told her that she deserved safety and protection, and that she was lovable. For Henry, looking into his fear told him that his prejudices against gay people were rooted in his childhood trauma with his step father and were not his own self definition. For Peggy, looking into her fear told her that she couldn't be all things to all people and that taking care of herself was paramount to her success. Her father's statement wasn't her perception of herself. For Betty, looking into her fear told her that she was lovable and her continued anger at others only kept her distanced from what she wanted most—connection.

Stop, look and listen is a gift and a valuable opportunity to take a look within

Look into your fear. What is it telling you about yourself? Listen. You will write it down in the Workbook section.

Biting Ben

Ben bit his nails down to the quick and until they bled. People would notice his mangled fingers. Sometimes he made excuses like he was planting in the yard all weekend, or he was sanding a piece of furniture. Ben was clearly embarrassed by his bad habit.

An advertising executive who was exceptionally successful and busy, as well as very much in the public eye, and for all his success and track record, Ben was a nervous wreck. When he overheard a new client mentioning his bad habit to the administrative assistant, Ben decided he really needed to **Just Stop Doing That**.

Ben revealed his history. He grew up in a military family. His father was an officer in the Marines and his mother stayed at home to raise the children. His father was adamant that Ben attend military school and following his father's footsteps into the Marines as his life's path. Ben, on the other hand, wanted to attend the local college with his friends and have a civilian life.

When his father heard of Ben's decision, he came down hard on him, expressing extreme disappointment in his choice and withholding funds for Ben's college education. Additionally, when Ben's father saw that he was not changing his mind, he enlisted the mother's support and both parents emotionally cut Ben off from the family, sending him to college with no family financial or emotional support.

Ben did well the first 2 years in college, but in his junior year, he became highly anxious and worried that he would never reunite with his parents. He began to fail classes and went home after fall semester with his tail between his legs, begging for forgiveness and joined the military.

Ben was tired of "hitting the wall" and wanted to come at this issue from a healthier perspective. After revealing his history, Ben recognized his Impasse as emotional abandonment and fear of unworthiness. Ben also acknowledged that he abandoned himself when he left college and joined the army reserves as this was his father's dream and not his own. He lived with an identity that wasn't his own creation and it made him extremely anxious and uncomfortable.

He let his father tell him his story rather than create his own. When he chose the advertising field, years after

his father's death, he continued to experience the fear of
unworthiness and bit his nails to distract himself from
his painful memories and fears. Ben desperately wanted
to **Just Stop Doing That!** He had a lot of work to do.

Once Ben recognized his Impasse, he was able to
forgive his father for imposing his dream on Ben. He was
also able to forgive himself for abandoning his dream in
order to reconnect to his family. Ben was often triggered
by feelings of anxiety and discomfort around his choice
of career, especially when Ben feared a client's discontent
with his advertising suggestions. Ben's bad habit,
biting his nails, distracted him from facing his fear of
abandonment by his clients.

Ben decided to stop his bad habit of biting his nails
the next time he felt afraid. Instead, he looked within
himself to identify and be with his fear of being unworthy. He listened to his higher thinking recognizing that he
always was and continues to be a worthy person who is
gifted and talented in his field. He became more and
more empowered to refrain from his habit. Eventually,
he started getting weekly manicures and felt very proud
of how his hands looked.

Stop, look and listen is a gift and a valuable opportunity to take a look within. As you do this, think about some
aspects of your identity that you really don't like; your
bad habit may be covering that negative self concept.
Stop judging yourself. Do you remember that judgments
only serve to keep you entrenched in your bad habit?

The fact that you distract yourself with a bad habit is neither bad nor good; it just is. What do you want to create for yourself around this situation? Consider acknowledging and responding to your inner fear. You are now empowered to notice it, reframe it as an Impasse, and then identify the judgment you have cast upon yourself because of it. When you are on the brink of engaging in a bad habit; *stop, look and listen*. You can then patiently identify what it is you need to be at peace and free of fear. Now, go for it and complete the connection to your peaceful point of view.

CHAPTER SIX

So *There* I Am!

Reconnecting to Your Spirit

Reconnecting to your spirit is finding all that was precious and innocent in you once again. Here is your moment of truth, the chance to be who you really are. Once you have completed the first four steps, this one is simple. You have relinquished judgment of yourself and others. You have used thoughts of peace and given over your fear to your spirit or higher mind. You are now ready to be one with your higher self.

This is the only step that requires you to do almost nothing! Just be still and calmly listen. Simply be present for yourself. You are no longer invested in the distracting behaviors of your bad habits. Having identified your historical grievances, you have moved beyond separation anxiety and you are ready to be the authentic you.

When you practice this over time, forgiveness tends to come to mind quickly and doesn't require much effort on your part.

This requires no concerted effort on your part except a calm, attentive, listening position. The things we most want and need are well within our reach. It is as if we attract them into our thinking. We are ready to be these things and with practice, we learn to remember who we are and those attributes are now and will remain the core of our identities.

Reconnecting to your spirit implies that you have released your past and have responded to your fears, as you applied the two steps of forgiveness. When you practice this over time, forgiveness tends to come to mind quickly and doesn't require much effort on your part. Think about how much energy you have poured into your bad habits that can now be directed into more productive states such as trust, honesty, tolerance, gentleness, joy, self-intimacy, generosity, patience, faithfulness, and open-mindedness. First you get to enjoy these characteristics for yourself. This will feel so wonderfully liberating and powerful that you will be enthusiastic to extend the same to others. You then will be able to co-create healthy spiritual alliances.

Initially, when you reconnect to your spirit and seem to be doing just fine, something will happen that will typically shoot you down and leave you vulnerable to relapse into your bad habit. When you begin to make your shift to the higher mind, you may first experience an intensification of fear as a way to bring you back to the familiarity of your prior distress and distraction. You might find yourself being seduced by fear to slip back into the distraction of your habit. At these times, you can explore and discover a vehicle for looking within to help you stay present and authentic.

Here are some activities, other than meditation or prayer that might work as ways to calm your mind and help you look within:

Practicing yoga
Being in nature
Engaging in the arts
Sending peace to the person you dislike
Reading and journaling
Cooking a meal
Stargazing
Helping the sick
Doing charitable acts
Taking care of children
Playing games
Helping the elderly
Reading for the blind
Participating in an ecological endeavor

Joining or forming a support group
Actively listening
Expressing gratitude

These are just some suggestions. You may have your own ideas in mind.

The habits that were given up in this book include:

Smoking: Samantha joined a support group and regularly attends Pilates. She no longer smokes.

Compulsive overeating: Harrison went to Overeaters Anonymous and became a Big Brother to an overweight child. Harrison has lost 130 pounds.

Procrastinating: Peggy took piano lessons which taught her to relax and focus. Incidentally, she was on time and prepared for every lesson.

Excessive Shopping: Susie found her honesty and told her husband the truth. He didn't leave her. Instead he helped her launch a thrift shop where she sold her stuff and gave half the profit to charity. She isn't shopping excessively any more. She became a buyer for a local department store.

Over-working: William realized that what really mattered to him were his relationships. He renewed his marital vows and cut his work week in half. He now works a 40-hour week.

Criticizing others: Henry became much more tolerant. He took up kayaking as a way to relax. He is now married with children and the coach of his son's soccer team.

Drinking too much: Allen stopped drinking, joined Alcoholics Anonymous and stays peaceful by being in nature at his cabin in the woods.

Negativity, nastiness, crankiness: Betty got some counseling. She also got a new job in the human resources department of a large company. Betty is well liked by her colleagues and started a bridge club with some people from work.

Nail biting: Ben stopped biting his nails and gets a manicure every week. His company is very successful and his clients love him.

Your habit may be complicated, or maybe it is simple and obvious. Once you have mastered the five simple steps of Rapid Advance, the nature of your habit really is not that important anymore.

When life's challenges trigger your historical upsets, you are at risk to feel afraid and then, distract yourself with a bad habit. When you remember forgiveness, **the relinquishment of judgment followed with a thought of peace,** you can notice your fear, rise above it to your spiritual perspective, stay centered and remain trustworthy of your ability to **JUST STOP DOING THAT!**

We wish you luck as you complete the Workbook. Please move through it slowly and deliberately so that you can take the precious time you deserve for creative introspection. Our hope is that after you move through the five simple steps of the Rapid Advance Process, you will develop some healthier points of view and some healing and healthy intentions for yourself.

Ellie and Vicki

PART TWO

The Rapid Advance
Workbook

THE FIVE STEPS OF
THE RAPID ADVANCE PROCESS

Relinquishment of Judgment
Thought of Peace

INTRODUCTION

We have been in the helping professions collectively for over 50 years. We have helped countless people face their challenges and faced our own. We all deserve to feel happy and fulfilled and too many of us put up with unnecessary pain for too long.

The *Rapid Advance Process* offered in this workbook will be the beginning of the most positive change in your life! Working through it will help you see yourself as whole and free from the pain of loss so you can get rid of your bad habits.

This workbook follows the book **Just Stop Doing That!**, an important resource for anyone who wants to stop distracting themselves from their true problems and lead a happy and fulfilling life. Please be sure to read the book before starting the workbook. Now, follow along with us, take your time, and use this guide in a way that will best serve your individual needs.

LOOKING AT YOURSELF
AS A PERSON

Do you feel internally calm and peaceful enough to handle the challenges of a breaking a bad habit?

_____

_____

_____

_____

Did anything traumatic happen to you in your life? (it doesn't have to be some big dramatic event; remember that trauma is in the eye of the beholder)

_____

_____

_____

_____

What does the word spirituality mean to you?

_____

_____

_____

_____

What puts a lump in your throat or makes you
really emotional?

_____

_____

_____

_____

Are you feeling satisfied with your family connections?
Explain why or why not.

_____

_____

_____

_____

Are you suffering with any chronic or intermittent
unexplained physical symptoms?

_____

_____

_____

_____

Are you sleeping well?

_____

_____

_____

_____

Do you worry?

_____

_____

_____

Are you happy?

_____

_____

_____

_____

Do you make time for your own personal enjoyment?

_____

_____

_____

_____

What do you do to relax?

_____

_____

_____

_____

_____

Do you think you can really get close to someone?

_____

_____

_____

_____

Do you want someone to get really close to you?

_____

_____

_____

_____

If you let someone get really close to you, what do you think (or fear) they would find out about you? Think about this question and write your truthful answer.

_____

_____

_____

_____

_____

_____

EXERCISE 1:

An Act of Courage

Write down five issues that seem to trigger the distraction of a bad habit.

1. _____

2. _____

3. _____

4. _____

5. _____

EXERCISE 2:

An Act of Faith

Write down five things that would be different and better for you if you allowed yourself to build your self-confidence and your skill at managing your strong emotions.

1. _____

2. _____

3. _____

4. _____

5. _____

THE RAPID ADVANCE PROCESS

After years of practice, we finally understand that struggling with letting go of a bad habit is really a distraction from dealing directly with the real problem. We also have reframed the use of a bad habit as the loss of connectedness to your higher thinking or spiritual self. When you approach life from the part of your brain that houses your higher mind, you can face fear, and do not see yourself as alone and powerless. You are then able to control your distracting behavior and get to the heart of the matter. You can recover.

Before you embark on this journey, let's first clear your mind of any negative or counterproductive notions of spirituality. Many of us were raised with religious practices that were either heavy handed or forced upon us. Others were raised with no spiritual practice at all. Some of us have simply allowed that part of our experience to waste away over time.

Exercise 1:

Please list below any negative connotations that the word 'spirituality' elicits for you.

_____

_____

_____

_____

_____

_____

_____

_____

_____

_____

_____

_____

_____

_____

_____

_____

_____

_____

_____

Exercise 2:

Make a list of the traits, characteristics, and behaviors you would like to create as you get rid of your bad habits and become more spiritual with yourself and in your relationships with others.

_____   _____

_____   _____

_____   _____

_____   _____

_____   _____

What would that part of you feel like?

_____

_____

_____

_____

How would that part be of assistance to you when you are tempted by your distraction? Please do not rush through this section.

_____

_____

_____

_____

We are now ready to proceed with the Rapid Advance Process. By completing the next five chapters you will have the opportunity to mend, build and strengthen a strong connection to yourself. In so doing, you will have the opportunity to develop a reliable practice of accessing your own remarkable internal resources.

The Rapid Advance Process consists of five steps for getting rid of bad habits:

1. **Reveal Your History**

2. **Recognize Your Impasse**

3. **Release Your Past**

4. **Respond to Your Fear**

5. **Reconnect with Your Higher Thinking**

Please remember this is not a substitute for treatment for recovered memories of traumatizing events earlier in one's life. This process is for personal growth and getting rid of bad habits. If you are an adult survivor of serious <u>untreated</u> childhood trauma, it is imperative that you seek appropriate treatment for your psychological injuries.

Reveal Your History

It Was

You may think that your history has nothing significant in it that triggers or upsets you. Nonetheless, a part of your brain relays every memory you ever experienced and at the most inopportune times. Whether your fears from childhood are a dark closet, being bullied by a scary kid, getting caught in the rain, coming home from school and having no one in the house, hearing strange noises, having nightmares, losing a friend, losing a love, accidents, feeling publicly embarrassed in school or in front of the family, becoming ill and missing out on important activities, surgery, hospital stays, shyness, moving, just to name a few; they are stored. These "historical feeling states" can be triggered in our present-day relationships. Having an awareness of your historical hot buttons is crucial in the maintenance of your emotional and spiritual well-being and helping get rid of your bad habits.

EXERCISE 1:

The following questions will help build your awareness of historical feeling states and/or experiences that may seem as normal events to you but may get triggered in the course of your life. You may also have significant recollection of events but you may not have an awareness of the body memories and the gut-feelings associated with these memories. You may even think you have dealt with some of these memories and laid them to rest. We now ask you to reconsider them in this new context. Doing so may help you get rid of your bad habits.

As you move through the exercises below, be patient. Go slowly and look within yourself in a gentle and self-accepting manner. The purpose of revealing your history is not to judge or evaluate; it is simply to honor and acknowledge.

YOUR PARENTS, YOUR FAMILY AND YOUR WORDLY ATTACHMENTS

Describe your early memories of your mother with five descriptive words.

1. _____

2. _____

3. _____

4. _____

5. _____

Describe your early memories of your father with five descriptive words.

1. _____
2. _____
3. _____
4. _____

Did your family suffer a life altering event such as a death or divorce? Write down what it was.

_____

_____

_____

_____

How was this addressed in your family?

_____

_____

_____

_____

If you lived in a blended family (or step family) please describe what this experience was like for you.

_____

_____

_____

_____

Imagine watching an old movie of yourself as a child.
Describe what you see.

_____

_____

_____

_____

_____

_____

Describe your parents' marriage with five descriptive
words:

1. _____

2. _____

3. _____

4. _____

5. _____

How did your parents/step-parents resolve their conflicts?
What did you see? What did you hear or not hear?

_____

_____

_____

_____

_____

How did you feel when your parents/step-parents were having conflicts?

_____

_____

_____

_____

How did you feel when conflicts went unaddressed?

_____

_____

_____

_____

How did your parents/step-parents handle issues around money?

_____

_____

_____

_____

How did your parents/step-parents handle issues around religion?

_____

_____

_____

_____

How did your parents/step-parents handle issues
around food?

_____

_____

_____

_____

How did your family have fun together?

_____

_____

_____

_____

How was affection displayed in your family?

_____

_____

_____

_____

How were issues around sex approached in your family?

_____

_____

_____

_____

How was illness addressed in your family?

_____

_____

_____

_____

Was there any addiction or substance abuse in your family? How did it you affect you?

_____

_____

_____

_____

What was the role of extended family in your life?

_____

_____

_____

_____

How were you disciplined?

_____

_____

_____

_____

How were your relationships with your siblings?
What was your birth order?

_____

_____

_____

_____

What are your most vivid memories?

_____

_____

_____

_____

What were your greatest joys as a child?

_____

_____

_____

_____

What scared you as a child?

_____

_____

_____

_____

What were some ways you used to distract yourself when you felt afraid or upset? Some examples might be day-dreaming, thumb sucking, nail biting, masturbating, nightmares, bed wetting, temper tantrums, withdrawal, bullying, underachieving, over-achieving, lying or crying.

_____

_____

_____

_____

_____

How did you get attention?

_____

_____

_____

_____

Did you have any behavioral problems as a child?

_____

_____

_____

_____

Did you have any particular challenges in growing up that stand out in your memory such as poverty, illness, learning disabilities, disappointments, deaths, divorce, etc?

_____

_____

_____

_____

YOUR EDUCATIONAL EXPERIENCES

Describe your experience in elementary school.

_____

_____

_____

_____

Describe your experience in middle school.

_____

_____

_____

_____

Describe your experience in high school.

_____

_____

_____

_____

Did you change schools while you were growing up? If so, how often?

_____

_____

_____

_____

If you moved, how did it affect your relationships?

_____

_____

_____

_____

How did your parents explain the moves?

_____

_____

_____

_____

How did your family communicate about important life changes?

_____

_____

_____

_____

_____

Describe any other significant relationships that you had while growing up: friendships, romance, relationships with grandparents, aunts, uncles, teachers or other authority figures, peer groups, extracurricular activities you participated in, etc.

EXERCISE 2:

Write a story of the first time you felt afraid and distracted yourself. What was your distraction?

EXERCISE 3:

What patterns do you see emerging as you reveal certain aspects of your history? How you developed and evolved is important to how you cope today. Our goal here is that these patterns and coping mechanisms become identifiable to you.

Examples of patterns that you may identify are Avoidant, Passive, Aggressive, Passive-Aggressive, Abusive, Neglectful, Overprotective, Depressed, Anxious, Disconnected, Numb, Silent, Addictive, Oppositional, Bystanding, Perfectionistic, etc. You may come up with a pattern of your own that is not mentioned here. No one knows your history better than you do!

EXERCISE 4:

After revealing your history, identify and write down some
judgments, opinions and evaluations you began to make
about yourself and your place in the world as you moved
through the early developmental stages of life. For example, a child who had a chronically ill mother may have
judged themselves as abandoned and alone, or seen
themselves as a caretaker for that parent, or as a "stand-in
spouse" for the other parent. Another example is an adopt-
ed child may have frequently felt sad because they judged
themselves as an outsider or perhaps felt disconnected
from the rest of the family. A child of addictive parents may
have judged themselves as unworthy of attention
and regard because the parents appeared more interested
in the addictive substance (e.g. alcohol, drugs, gambling)
than they were in the child. A child of divorce may
have judged themselves as the cause of the divorce and
therefore, not lovable enough to keep the family intact.

These types of self-judgments, while untrue, are
likely conclusions for a child to draw because at an early
stage of development, a child is naturally tends to
perceive him/herself as the center of the universe.
As adults, it is our wish for you to begin to identify and
address these faulty core beliefs.

Below, write down the judgments you made about
yourself as a child growing up in the context of your
family. Add the distracting behavior you used to cope
with these feelings and judgments.

Recognizing Your Impasse

It Is

History repeats itself. Even history that we don't recall repeats itself. Revealing your history is an empowering first step. Now we would like you to consider how you might unwittingly re-create some early patterns in your adult life. We are referring to the patterns that you have already identified in the preceding chapter. Those of us who have unconscious and/or unresolved fears and judgments about ourselves are at risk to repeat the pattern in our adult life.

The Impasse is defined as an emotional and physiological fear reaction; a fear reaction that has its roots in our history. This reaction has three dimensions: 1) the memory itself; 2) the negative feeling you have attached to it; and 3) the judgment you have made about yourself and the others involved in it. When triggered, you continue to distract yourself, believing the distraction to be a form of self protection, when in reality the only thing that is being protected is the historical fear itself. *The unconscious purpose of defending your Impasse is to protect yourself from ever having to feel the fear that originated in early childhood.* Children normally find ways to distract themselves from feeling afraid simply because fear is an overwhelming feeling in the experience of a child. A child does not yet possess the thinking skills or the internal tools to manage their fears.

As an adult, rather than resort to distracting behaviors, or bad habits, which are generally destructive; you need to recognize the historical fear, turn into it, and overcome it. Until now, you have used various distractions to avoid feeling afraid. Your goal now is to no longer distract yourself. You deserve and need to recognize the personal distraction you're using which covers your original fear. You are now ready to move into the fear and not into the distraction. Recognize the originating fear and identify it. We will call this your Impasse.

The self-protective distractions of your childhood mature as you developed. Now that you have revealed your history, you are able to become conscious about and recognize how you find yourself at your own Impasse repeatedly thought your bad habits in adulthood.

EXERCISE 1:

Let us recognize how this step applies to you. Think again and repeat the identification of childhood distractions/ coping mechanisms you utilized when you felt afraid. List them below.

EXERCISE 2:

Now think about the more adult behaviors that you do today that might be considered "evolved distractions" of your childhood reactions to fear. For example, a thumb-sucker or a nail biter may now be a cigarette smoker; a shy child may be a socially withdrawn adult; a child that used illness for attention may be chronically ill as an adult; an overachiever may turn into a workaholic; a bully might grow up to struggle with road rage. List the adult distractions you use below.

_____

_____

_____

_____

_____

_____

_____

When you peel away the distractions, you might notice that you are experiencing anxiety. The anxiety you feel when you stop distracting yourself is a form of separation anxiety, emptiness or a void resulting from being in disconnect from the spiritual part of your personality. All children have some form of anxiety when they feel afraid because their little brains have yet to develop the cerebral cortex or that area of the brain that is responsible for higher thinking or rational thought. So you are not alone with this anxiety. Everyone has it in one form or another. Now that you know this, you can move forward and learn how to have it, so that it doesn't have you.

As an adult, you now have developed this part of your brain which needs to be more regularly accessed as a healthy coping mechanism for dealing with fear. Training our brains to move into this higher functioning is derailed when we continue to distract with childhood coping mechanisms rather than adult responses. Our goal is to open the spiritual bridge or neural pathway to your spiritual mind and that part of your higher brain.

EXERCISE 3:

It is now time to think about and write down some situation where you found yourself feeling particularly uncomfortable or that evoked a physical sensation or "gut kick" in your body. Gut kicks are warnings that feelings are being triggered, such as anger, fear or sadness. Use the lines below for this exercise.

_____

_____

_____

_____

_____

_____

_____

_____

_____

_____

_____

Recognize when you are playing an updated version of an historical scene in your life and allow yourself to experience rather than avoid the unpleasant separation anxiety that gets triggered in the replay. When you remain unconscious of your Impasse, you will find yourself in situations that trigger it again and again. You need to allow yourself to experience the legitimate anxiety in order to heal. Write down something from your personal history that you unconsciously replay over and over in your life that triggers your bad habit.

_____

_____

_____

_____

_____

_____

_____

Now, say to yourself:

- Something is getting triggered in me.
- This is not about my current situation.
- This is about what my current life situation is triggering from my own personal history.
- It's okay that I am feeling this.
- I will not judge it.
- I will remain calm so that I may identify what is coming to the surface.
- By identifying and becoming conscious of it, I will take better care of myself.
- I don't have to react the way I did as a child.
- I am an adult now and have other choices
- I do not have to distract myself from this upset in order to survive.

- Instead, I need to feel what I am feeling, move through it, and remember the memory that is being triggered is in the past and does not have to hold any meaning for me in the present.
- It is powerless over me today.

Write down the subjects that trigger your Impasses:

(Some examples might be childhood violence, molestation, abandonment, corporal punishment, divorce, death of a family member, death of a child, moving, an angry father/mother, a passive mother/father, peer rejection, failure at something you attempted, bullying, cheating, accidents, foul weather, illness, addictions, neglect, certain words, the parental "look", etc.)

_____

_____

_____

_____

Put your Impasse into words into the space below. Remember, your Impasse contains your memory of the event, the feelings you had about the event when it happened and how you judged or evaluated yourself or others involved in light of the event.

_____

_____

_____

No one knows your Impasse better than you. Develop an inner of awareness of your Impasse and make friends with it. Don't avoid it any more. Right now we ask you to recognize it so you can move forward and think peacefully about it. Imagine letting go of a painful part of your past so that it no longer has power to scare you or make you sad. Imagine how strong you will feel when you no longer have to distract yourself from your true feelings because you have mastered your ability to experience them.

Release Your Past

I Can

Your unconscious attachment to some parts of your past prohibit you from bridging to the higher mind or spiritual self, which is the most powerful and peaceful part of you. When that part of you is present, you can stay peacefully centered in the here and now. Having identified your Impasse and deciding no longer to retreat from it, you can now begin to mend the break in your spiritual bridge. By releasing your painful perception of the past, you can stop protecting an historical fear and heal your connection to hope and peacefulness. You are now beginning to successfully connect or bridge to your higher mind and access the power of your spiritual self. This will empower you to stop your bad habit and create peacefulness in your life without the unwanted distractions.

In releasing the past you must remember that your memories don't equal the past. What you remember is far less impacting than *how* you remember it. The historical action itself is over. It is only your judgment of yourself and others in its context that remains. For example, if you have a memory of being disciplined by an aggressive parent, there may be a childlike part of you that remembers this event with embarrassment or shame. You may believe, in some way, you were not worthy of receiving love. The memory itself is far less damaging than your perception or judgment of who you are in light of it. So, think of this possibility: when you get triggered in the here and now by a life event, and you want to distract with your bad habit, you can heal your perception of a painful historical event anytime you choose to relinquish judgment of that event.

EXERCISE 1:

Review in writing the historical events that you identified as Impasses in Step 2.

_____

_____

_____

_____

Identify the feelings you had with those particular Impasse memories. (Painful memories might typically bring up a feeling of sadness, embarrassment, shame, disappointment, anger and/or fear. These feelings, left unattended, may generate a personal sense of inadequacy in you which can be the trigger for your use of a bad habit.

_____

_____

_____

_____

_____

_____

_____

_____

_____

List the judgments or negative thoughts you made about yourself or others around these Impasse events. For example: "I was a bad girl because my father was always angry" or "I was unlovable because no one paid attention to me."

_____

_____

_____

_____

_____

_____

_____

_____

_____

_____

_____

_____

_____

_____

_____

_____

_____

_____

_____

EXERCISE 2:

In order to rid yourself of these judgments and faulty beliefs, you now need to exchange your fear for forgiveness.

Admit you have the fear. Write down what you are afraid of. (ex., I have a fear of not being good enough, of being stupid, embarrassed, etc.)

_____

_____

_____

_____

_____

_____

Take personal responsibility for the role your memory is playing in your life and decide what it is you want to create around this memory. (ex., healing, peace, calmness, closure, release or forgiveness versus resentment, anger, hostility, grievance, continued pain, vengeance, depression, anxiety or physical illness.)

_____

_____

_____

_____

_____

_____

Realize the negative judgment or faulty thinking you associate with the historical event and on the person or persons in the event with you. List these counterproductive thoughts, perceptions and judgments.

_____

_____

_____

_____

_____

_____

_____

Remove all descriptive words that depict the event. For example rather than say "My father was a disgusting drunk and I hated him!" say instead, "My father drank too much and sometimes I felt afraid of him."

_____

_____

_____

_____

_____

_____

_____

Remove all your judgments, unconsciously made at an earlier time, from the description of the event. Commit to exchange your fear around this event with forgiveness; forgiveness of yourself and forgiveness of the others who were involved. _You do not have to forgive the event itself. The event may not have been okay_. You are forgiving yourself and the other people involved so you can be released from the painful memory. Remember, this forgiveness is not for them- it is for **you** to be free. It is through your forgiveness of the other person that you can be released from a painful past.

_____

_____

_____

_____

_____

_____

_____

_____

Write on the lines below, I forgive... (ex., my father for being an alcoholic) and I forgive myself for... (ex., believing I wasn't lovable enough for him to stop drinking).

_____

_____

_____

_____

Forgiveness is for people not for actions. For example spanking is an action; because you were spanked doesn't mean you were bad. Maybe you engaged in behavior that was unacceptable; that doesn't mean you are unacceptable. You made a mistake, you are not a mistake.

EXERCISE 3:

What stands in your way when you think about forgiveness (ex., some people see themselves as justified in carrying grievances)?

In deciding to release the past, you can move from fear to forgiveness. Forgiveness is the release of judgment followed by peaceful thoughts. You can now remember that in light of a painful memory, you remain worthy of compassion and regard. The thoughts of peace will now serve you in your next step, responding to fear.

Respond To Your Fear

I Know

There is a big difference between responding and reacting. Reacting involves little or no spiritual connection.
It is based on the primitive brain's instinct of fight, flight
or freeze and is defensive in nature. You react when
you perceive the need to protect yourself. If you take
yourself back to the first step, you'll remember that you
are invested in protecting yourself from feeling historical
fears. To do so is faulty thinking and a dangerous place
to put yourself when you are looking to rid yourself of
bad habits.

Responding involves the introduction of a reply or an
answer and is associated with the conscious left brain.

Take a second and consider how you tend to react in emotionally charged or fearful conditions in your relationships. Some possibilities are perfectionism, procrastination, rage, impatience and silence.

Once you have relinquished or given over the self-judgment unconsciously made at a much earlier time, you need to stay peaceful when you meet up with your fears in life. For example, if your father drank too much and you sometimes felt afraid of him, it doesn't follow that you see yourself as unlovable because he wasn't more responsive to you as a lovable child. Your father's drinking was about him and his own self-abandonment. You always deserved to have a present, attentive father. The fact that your father didn't step up to his parental responsibilities wasn't bad or good. It just was. Because it wasn't bad or good, you can now respond when these feelings are triggered. Responding, rather than reacting, implies thinking peacefully or calmly when you are deciding what to do or what to say in that fear-provoking situation. Responding rather than reacting to emotional fear is the most important part of getting rid of your bad habits. Responding is a discipline. It requires a lot of mental structure and practice in order to become proficient at it.

Now that you have revealed your history, recognized your Impasse and made a commitment to release the past, you are ready to respond to the historical fear that gets triggered in your daily life today and leads you to your bad habits.

EXERCISE 1:

Stop, Look and Listen

Do you remember this phrase being taught to you as a child when you were learning to cross the street? Some streets are easier to cross than others. At some of the dangerous intersections, you could easily be mowed down if you didn't adhere to the rule. When you find yourself at a scary emotional intersection in your work, the rule of responding is to stop, look and listen.

Stop: Identify what will become your personal red light. What was once a burden in your distraction from fear can now serve you as a blessing in that it signals something is being triggered for you. Simply stop. What is your adult distraction when you feel afraid? Here are some possibilities: raging, numbing out, drinking, drugs, withdrawing, isolating, stealing, shopping, dissociating, impatience, passivity, eating disorders, working too much, headaches, stomach aches, ringing in the ears, intrusive thoughts, nightmares, sleeping, fuzzy thinking, biting your nails or forgetting to breathe. What are yours? Keep in mind that it could be more than one symptom.

Look: look inside and become introspective and think about what is being triggered in your history? Acknowledge it. Honor it. Relinquish judgment about yourself and others involved. Think peacefully about it. Forgive it. For example, if your fear of not being good enough is being triggered by your boss at work, and you have stopped the distracting behaviors you used to engage in to mask the pain, you have now freed yourself to look inward and reveal your truth as to what is happening.

Listen: Listen to your inner voice and your inner truth. Think back to what you wrote in the previous steps.

EXERCISE 1:

Write about a time when you turned to your bad habit. Identify what was triggering something deeply personal for you. As you write it, you can listen peacefully to your inner story and remember that this is about *you* and not about the use of your bad habit; it is about your upset. The upset belongs to you and you need to be accountable for it. Then, realize you deserve to forgive, to be forgiven and to be more patient with yourself and anyone else who was involved. Write your story using "I" statements and conclude with the statement: "May this story rest in peace".

Practice the two forgiveness steps of releasing judgment followed by peaceful thoughts. On the lines below, make a forgiveness list for hurts you have incurred in your life. Every story is an opportunity for practicing forgiveness. Remember; to err is human; to forgive is divine.

Make a list of all the people you want to forgive and also include the things for which you wish to be forgiven.

_____   _____

_____   _____

_____   _____

_____   _____

_____   _____

_____   _____

_____   _____

_____   _____

_____   _____

_____   _____

_____   _____

_____   _____

_____   _____

_____   _____

This practice is universally healing and the person doing the forgiving is successfully bridging or connecting to his/her higher mind, creating new-found hope, faith and trust in one's own ability to create healthy patterns of behavior.

Reconnect To Your Spirit

I Am

This is the most rewarding part of the process. There is nothing you have to do. There is nothing you have to figure out. Simply let your mind be still. Now that you are no longer distracted, anxious, worried or fearful, you have opened the way to clear your mind and connect to your higher self where you receive the characteristics or traits of higher mind thinking. This allows you to bring these traits into your life, stop your bad habits, and attract more positive behaviors and people in your life.

Now that you are no longer distracted and can let your mind be still, you are empowered to start engaging in some activities which will allow wisdom, calm and peaceful thoughts into your mind and your relationships. Let your mind receive and connect to them. Find some activities to strengthen the connection: meditation, prayer, nature hikes, gardening, 12-step programs, playing sports, running, engaging in the arts, reading, journaling, playing games, expressing gratitude, yoga, joining an encouragement group, dancing and cooking are only a few options. You'll meet great people through these activities who are also invested in connecting this way. Develop a spirituality/peace plan: something that you will do daily, weekly, monthly to clear your mind and allow the spiritual traits to come into your thinking. Put it on your calendar. Schedule it in pen.

EXERCISE 1:

List some loving qualities you want to nurture within yourself, so that you can see them clearly and not distract away from your goals.

EXERCISE 2:

Write down all the things that you wish you had the time to do and haven't been able to fit into your schedule. This can be your own personal bucket list.

EXERCISE 3:

Make five affirmations that you can repeat—one for each day of the work week. For example:

- I am going to be more tolerant and patient with myself and others.

- I want to be aware of and connected to my own feelings so that I can be accountable for them in my life.

- I am grateful for the blessings I have and the love I can give.

- I will be introspective or do some soul-searching today. I will think of any upsetting situations that have occurred so far and address them with the Process I have learned instead of distracting myself.

- Today I will nurture myself.

- This week, there have been satisfying and taxing experiences in my life. I have learned some important things about myself. I will use this information to grow.

- I have stayed in the present and not allowed my past to dictate my use of bad habits.

- I have not been distracted with bad habits. I have replaced fear with faith.

Today I have Just Stopped Doing That!

Now, write your own.

1. _____

2. _____

3. _____

4. _____

5. _____

Commit to follow through with your plan. On this last page write a contract beginning with the line: "I hereby enter into this agreement with myself..." Sign and date your agreement. Refer back to it frequently to remember your agreement and to stay the course.

ABOUT THE AUTHORS

Ellie Izzo, PhD, LPC

Ellie has been in clinical practice for over 30 years. She also serves as a trainer, Divorce Coach and Child Specialist in Collaborative Divorce cases. She developed the Rapid Advance Process, a standardized five-session brief model of counseling that was presented at the American Counseling Association convention in Atlanta in 1997 and with Vicki Carpel Miller in Honolulu in 2008. Ellie is the author of The Bridge To I Am, a self-help book outlining the Rapid Advance Process used in the treatment of Vicarious Trauma and other life challenges. Ellie hosted a call-in radio show in Phoenix and served as Self-Help Editor for a nationally syndicated trade magazine.

She runs several ongoing groups called the Encouragers where people meet to offer each other peace, support and acceptance. She is Co-Director of the Vicarious Trauma Institute and the Collaborative Divorce Institute, based in Scottsdale, Arizona.

Vicki Carpel Miller, BSN, MS, LMFT

Vicki Carpel Miller is a licensed Marriage and Family Therapist in clinical practice for over 20 years. She is co-founder and Co-Director of the Vicarious Trauma Institute and the Collaborative Divorce Institute, both located in Scottsdale, Arizona. Vicki was instrumental in bringing Collaborative Divorce to Arizona and functions as a Divorce Coach and Child Specialist in Collaborative Divorce cases. She specializes in the treatment of Vicarious Trauma, the Rapid Advance Process, the practice of Collaborative Divorce and other divorce-related issues such as blended family and stepfamily issues. Vicki is internationally recognized as a trainer with the Collaborative Divorce Training Team, the Collaborative Divorce Institute and the Vicarious Trauma Institute. Her offices are located in Scottsdale, Arizona.

Read all of Vicki and Ellie's titles
in the Just Stop series

Just Stop Doing That!

Just Stop Picking Losers!

Just Stop Eating That!

AND COMING IN 2012

Just Stop Saying That!

Just Stop Fighting!

Just Stop Freaking Out!

Order your copies at: www.hcipress.com

Visit the author's website at:
www.vicarioustrauma.com

Contact them to speak at your next event or training:
collaborate119@aol.com
ellieizzo9@yahoo.com

CPSIA information can be obtained at www.ICGtesting.com
Printed in the USA
BVOW010832031011

272639BV00003B/2/P

9 781936 268221